THE FINAL COUNTDOWN TO DOOM HAS BEGUN
By Freddie L. Sirmans, Sr.

The stupid thing about becoming too government dependent in a free country is sooner or later every government is going to run out of money, or the ability to borrow.

The USA is almost there, good men has stood by and let the liberals create this welfare state beast that has destroyed our nuclear family system, our breadbasket small farmers, and lastly any emergency capacity to barter.

Those things are the basic of every civilized society and for their loss the USA is going to pay dearly in pain, suffering, and starving. The great wisdom found in Freddie L. Sirmans, Sr's books and writings lay out the wisest course to take.

Privatizing government out of its super social and family provider role is the first thing that must be done. Next, the minimum wage must be completely eliminated and all taxes cut to the bone that will then set entrepreneurs free to feed and save America.

I have too much wisdom and common sense to be taken serious in this insane economic atmosphere, my great wisdom and sound judgment will be written off as the ranting and raving of a lunatic.

I say to hell with the party line and following any be happy economic propaganda over a cliff, because if we stay on the course we are on America will not survive.

Anyone with an ounce of economic wisdom will know that I'm right. Actually, the jig is up. If we don't move fast and get out front on this, nature's law of "Natural selection" will do it its way, which is cold, brutal, and unforgiving.

HOW TO CREATE JOBS!
With my great wisdom I will give you a very simple answer that has withstood the test of time and is guaranteed to work. Jobs are created by those with the funds and resources who want to and expect to make a profit.

If you take away any one of those ingredients jobs won't be created. The biggest culprit that is hindering job creation is big government by taxing away job producing business profit.

Making a profit is the only thing that can generate wealth. Sure, power can take from others or make others work for free and acquire wealth but only profit can generate wealth.

The problem with the USA economy and the global economy is it is like a vehicle with no reverse and that is stupid; no one would buy a car with no reverse.

That has created a false conception in most Americans that more and more money is the answer, wrong. It is not the amount of money but the buying power of money that is most important.

If it takes $50.00 to buy what we use to buy for $5.00 we have lost ground instead of gained ground in terms of buying power which is like a dog chasing his own tail, dumb, dumb, dumb, stupid, stupid, stupid, read Freddie L. Sirmans, Sr's books and writing on how to save America.

Big Government as a social and family provider has locked the USA and Europe into a global economic system that requires higher and higher taxes to support bigger and bigger government in a never ending inflationary spiral.

Around and around it goes with each tax increase cutting deeper and deeper into a business's profit until nothing is left. Plus, as government gets bigger and bigger the red tape hurdle on getting into business becomes almost insurmountable.

While all of this is going on you have masses

of people bitching and moaning wondering why there are no jobs. Yet, these same people keep voting the big spending liberals back in office to take care of everybody. Guess what, all personal and government income comes from some form of business profit.

It is very simple, the harder it is for a business to make a profit, the harder it is for people to find jobs. Also, the more business profit the government takes the fewer businesses can survive to provide tax paying jobs.

The end result is it is impossible for government to survive very long as a social and family provider, period. There is simply no way a welfare state can survive over 80-100 years, the drag and load becomes impossible to carry.

These same people think I'm stupid and uncaring when I say completely get rid of the minimum wage and kick the government out of its social and family provider role.

They forget the first priority is food, shelter, and staying warm. And no civilization has ever been able to do that without a strong nuclear and extended family system, along with adequate bartering capacity in small farmers and home gardeners, which our sugar daddy welfare state has almost destroyed.

A healthy free market place economy should be able to seek its own level like a liquid. By government invading the free market place and propping up prices that is what put prices out of reach for almost everyone, otherwise the poor with their numbers along would halt inflation.

This economy is about to crash but don't expect anything to change. Practically our whole culture and way of thinking now is to look to the government instead of to self, the nuclear and extended family, and lastly the government.

Until the "New deal" came about around eighty years ago, going back over 5,000 years people depended on themselves, the nuclear and extended family, the church, the community, and almost never on government to survive.

You can get into ideology, different types of government, or whatever, but unless there is a profit incentive no economic system is going to work, there are no exceptions in the history of man kind. I predict mass starving in the USA and around the world soon. However, I pray that I'm wrong.

The reason why liberals will always destroy wealth and freedom in a country is because their shallow do good intention makes them want to take all risk and failure out of life.

The shallow naive flaw in that type of thinking is human's beings is not cogs in a machine we are motivated by a complex reward or punishment response behavior. It is a law of nature that success and failure goes hand in hand and you can't have one without the other.

Just as it is as important to be able to forget things as it is to remember things but hardly anyone thinks about it that way, all of the focus is on remembering. So, when big government and the liberals prevent small purges and failures it puts the whole system at risk.

That shuts off any way to control inefficiency, crud, moral decay, and all negative anti-survival forces. Then it is only a matter of time before the negative forces of inefficiency and moral decay grow too powerful for human survival.

Also, it is impossible to create great wealth in a nation without someone willing to take a great risk and no one is going to be willing to take a great risk without individually expecting a great reward, liberals ignore this fact.

That is the reason communism and socialism

will never produce wealth and riches because everyone will try to exert the least amount of energy to receive an equal reward, and that is simply human nature.

What I've said is basic kindergarten human nature knowledge; still most liberals can't comprehend these facts. A hundred years ago just day to day survival made almost everyone aware of these fact, but not since the "New deal."

It is so sad just how shallow most Americans have become since the "New deal" and our all powerful sugar daddy welfare state has become the cradle to grave great white father super provider.

Soon when this great white father super provider is broke and has a red tape death grip on all self initiative, what are we to do? God help us break this death grip and survive.

God I ask in your name give us the wisdom and strength to survive in spite of what the well intention do good liberals has unknowingly done to this great country.

The technology to produce a vehicle that would cut fuel consumption almost in half has been around ever since the late 1950's. From an economically point of view there are thousands of things made from oil, from the pavement we drive on to the clothes on our backs, but fuel consumption is the lions share.

The reason no genuine serious effort to produce a mass fuel saving vehicle is not going to happen is because big business and the government wants more profit and revenue not less. Sure, there is some fiddling around and pretending to make a mass produced fuel saving vehicle but that is just throwing out a bone to fool the public.

If you think I'm wrong about a fuel saving vehicle take a look at the diesel locomotive. Two or three diesel locomotives can pull hundreds of box car all day long without gulping fuel. The reason is they have no drive train. The diesel engine powers a generator that supplies electrical power to electric motors for the wheels. And it's been that way ever since the late 1950's.

Sure, automobiles need quick acceleration for passing but with technology a way could be found to overcome that. All I'm saying is that in the real world what saves or works best don't always win out.

To sum it up, once the "New deal" gave the government an excuse to seize the nuclear family provider role for itself the destruction of the USA economy die was cast, estimated collapse time 4-6 generations into the future. As a super social and family provider the government is going to fight tooth and nails any and every decrease in revenue.

That is why government as a family provider will never allow a free people to remain free for very long. I have been out here screaming and hollering about the dangers of the welfare state to deaf ears now for many years.

But, I believe time is winding down and more and more my great wisdom is going to be realized and appreciated. I thank you God for my life, health, and strength. I carry on and refuse to stand down America.

I'm at a loss as how to think and act any other way. I give God the Praise, thank you God, thank you, thank you...

WRITERS OPINION ON STATES POWER!
I believe the main reason why the 10th amendment is totally ignored today is because of the passing of the 17th amendment. It wasn't obvious at the time but it has destroyed the balance of power between the federal government and the states.

In a real showdown the states no longer has any real power in congress because the senate is now mostly controlled by special interest. Without repealing the 17th amendment there is no stopping our welfare state beast created by liberals from both political parties.

Every day this beast is consolidating more and more power and soon states will be just designated regions. God I ask in your name, save this last bastion of true freedom in the world today, still the home of the brave, proud, and free.

OIL WELL WILD GOOSES CHASE!

Time is a wasting! I'm no oil man, and I'm no scientist, but I am a deep objective thinker. I believe time is wasting on what should have been done from the git go.

With escaping pressure around 2000 pounds per square inch over 5000 feet down only a relief well will allow a cap in my view. With that kind of pressure and that far down it is a no brainier that the pressure gotta be lowered before anything is gonna work. What do I know? We'll see, time is a wasting.

ECONOMIC UNDERSTANDING

It still amazes me of the lack of basic economic understanding that most Americans has or presumed to have.

Today I heard someone say that the tax payers won't have to foot the bill for the BP oil spill because BP make tons of profit and can well afford to pay. Hog wash, poppycock, BP don't have that kind of money, that kind of money can only come from BP raising oil prices then we all are gonna pay.

ARIZONA IMMIGRATION LAW
I'm so sick and tired of hearing supposedly intelligent people believing that this or that official hasn't read the Arizona immigration law. My God! That is one of the oldest lawyer tricks in the book.

One of the hardest things there is is to get a lawyer to admit having read anything unless it is in his/her best interest. Of course, they all have read the Arizona immigration law, but you can't prove it and question someone on something they don't know anything about. Case closed.

IMMIGRATION HYPOCRITES GALORE!
I'm going to give you the cold steel or rock hard facts on immigration because no one else is going to say it out loud. The first fact is it will be impossible to solve the immigration symptom and I say symptom because the welfare state is the root problem.

All I hear is a lot of hypocritical nonsense on

the subject and no one wanting to face cold hard facts. The USA can't feed itself or survive if it had to depend only on Americans to do field work and many other hard labor jobs.

Sure, I hear a lot of talk to the otherwise that is cheap, but try to tell a farmer with his harvest rotting in the field that kind of nonsense. You may not agree with me but I'll tell you how to solve the immigration problem, kick the welfare state the hell out of its super sugar daddy social and family provider role. And send it back to its designated role of collecting taxes, and protecting and defending the country.

As long as we have our existing welfare state it is futile and a waste of time and grandstanding for any politician to talk about solving the immigration symptom.

Far too many able bodied men in America don't have to work and especially doing hard labor, they can always sponge off of a mother, sister, aunt, or grandmother that is on the dole. For God sake, give me a break America.

President Ronald Wilson Reagan only had to deal with 3 millions illegals and here we are around 30 years later and around 30 millions illegals and guess what, many of the same people are still around singing the same old cop-out blues.

For God sake, give these people season work permits so they can come and go as they please and stop being hypocrites and face reality. They won't go home now because they are afraid they can't come back and work, a work permit is the only sensible thing to do.

Otherwise, they won't go home and in a few years we'll have 50 million and the same old song will still be playing and nothing will have changed as long as this welfare state has any say.

Europe doesn't have the illegal immigration problem like in the USA. The reason is they use a common sense approach like a guest worker permit.

However, something so simple and reasonable will never happen in the USA because the liberals are more interesting in gaining new voters to keep them in power than solving the problem.

WRITERS OPINION ON PUTTING ETHANOL IN GASOLINE!

I think putting ethanol in gasoline was one of the cruelest hoaxes ever pulled on the American people. Anyone that have an older or any car that is seldom driven is going to have problems.

With ethanol in it gasoline deteriorates so rapid that the gas tank needs draining after a month or so if not used. Plus, sooner or later it is going to drive the cost of all corn products out of sight.

I have an old classic car that I seldom drive and I gotta find me some ethanol free gasoline somewhere. Sometime later, shame on you Freddie Sirmans Sr, for thinking there is still individual freedom left in the USA to buy ethanol free gasoline!

Hell, how was I to know that it is mandated by the Feds that ethanol free gasoline can no longer be found in this great free country. I guess I will just have to drain all of the gas out of my old classic car and keep the tank empty or run the hell out of it. Wakeup America!

IS THE LIBERALS RUNNING A STALKING HORSE FOR THE UNITED STATES SUPREME COURT?

I have been wrong before and may be wrong on this. I just can't bring myself to believe that the liberals will actually vote anyone on to the United States Supreme Court that don't have a long established liberal ruling record.

In my mind it just doesn't add up, so I'm

going to call the bluff and up the ante. I think they want to soften up the opposition before sending in a die hard liberal with a long established liberal ruling record.

Remember folks, I'm just thinking out loud here I have no reason to think this except a gut feeling of my own. I just don't trust liberals with power. We'll see, Maybe they know something the rest of us don't that will trump a long proven liberal ruling record. However, my gut feeling is they don't and a stalking horse strategy is being used. There is no doubt about it, it is the roll of the dice on the part of the liberals, who really knows they probably hit the jackpot, but only history will give us the proof with a proven liberal ruling record

MR. GOVERNMENT! PLEASE BRING BACK THE GOLD, SILVER, OR PRECIOUS METAL SELF-CONTAINED VALUE-WITHIN-ITSELF REAL MONEY

These guys on TV were talking about spending and one made the point that government spending money comes from businesses and the taxpayers.

I agree, but, that is not the whole truth and nothing but the truth. You want the real truth! I'll give it to you! All government income originates from some form of business profit.

"Profit" and nothing but profit can create wealth. When you tax choke to death the goose that lays the golden egg you go to the poor house or you starve. However, you can never get a liberal to understand that simple fact.

The problem with economics is not enough Americans understand it not even trained economist. The first rule is you can't separate the economy from culture and human behavior.

The next thing is using money is supposed to be only an easier means of trading and bartering, societies survived with trading and bartering long before money or a currency was invented.

Actually, the value of money is supposed to be in the money itself in the form of gold, silver, or some other precious metal, not some worthless paper backed only on faith.

It started when someone suggested why carry around all of this heavy money why not let the government print a paper note and lock the gold and silver away as a backup.

That worked just fine until the "New deal" came along and opened the door for the government to seize the traditional family provider role for itself.

Once government got a taste of the God like power of being a super sugar daddy provider the politicians went hog wild and is still spending like there is no tomorrow.

The gold backup did survive until President Richard M. Nixon just flat outright outlawed it, then the liberals from both political parties with little or no resistance found themselves in spending hog heaven and are still having a field day.

Life itself is a process of cycles and rebirths, success and failure are part of our existence and there is absolutely nothing man can do to change that fact.

That means booms, busts, good times, hard times, famines, and horrible acts of nature are always going to come around sooner or later. The only tried and true protection that has allowed man and civilization to survive over the years is to maintain and safeguard a strong culture.

A strong culture must have a strong nuclear and extended family system, a strong religious or moral code in place, and adequate backup bartering capacity, we have very little of that left.

A physical valued or gold backed currency will safe guard a nations culture by purging or holding at bay the negative anti-survival forces like moral decay, left and right extremes, and porn.

Now, the only way to save the USA is to some how rebuild her culture, but that can never happen unless the people and the states vote the welfare state beast out of its super provider role.

I knew when the liberals finally got the elderly on government health care it was going to be almost impossible to save individual freedom and America itself. Once you make people your dependents very few are going to bite the hand that feeds them.

Now, nearly 50 percent of the American people are heavily government dependent and don't pay any federal income taxes, how can you expect people to vote against their own self interest, you can't.

The nation is on a suicide mission with little or no hope of individual freedom surviving, and even worse the young and average American still don't get it, especially the mostly liberal news media. Please God, help me educate this great nation.

This is a stress call for our survival as a free people. The big plus with getting back to a real physical currency with the value self contained within itself is it would assure survival of the people no matter how stupid the government acted.

The currency would be protected against all inflation and if you buried it or hid it under the mattress it would keep its value. Also, it would put most of the financial power back into the hands of the people.

I don't see any way USA sovereignty can be saved with the financial course we are on, the UN. or some world body will end up owning us if we don't get back to a real currency.

However, getting back to a real currency is something the people will have to demand because politicians and the government will never give up wielding their super provider God like power.

They will stop at nothing to continue trying to do the impossible which is to keep our welfare state beast fed. There is not enough money in the whole wide world to keep financing our welfare state, but the liberals are in complete denial and are taking the great USA down for the count.

Even today if you found a buried treasure hidden by a black beard over 600 years ago its value would be just as much because the value and worth is self-container within the precious metal itself.

WRITER SHARES SOME PERSONAL EXPERIENCE!

Freedom is something the average American takes for granted. While we sleep comfortable in our cozy warm beds at night very few of us ever take time to think that vigilantly standing guard every second twenty four hours everyday protecting us is our military.

It's been a long time now nearly fifty years ago when I was active duty military and played my small part physical and up close. I have seen up close some of the might that protects us.

The old Atlas ICBM's have long been retired now, but I have been down five floors deep into the bowels of a missile silo in the Nebraska countryside as a young U.S. Air Force firefighter.

Someone said something to this effect, "Freedom is never free."

God, I ask in your name save our great country.

THE POLITICAL DILEMMA OF A 3RD PARTY VOTE!

The thing about a 3rd party vote is there is no consolation prize it is an all of nothing game, and 99.9 percent of the time nothing is what one gets.

Everybody knows that a 3rd party movement only guarantees victory to the opposing major party, that is a given, there is no getting around that fact.

So, I say concede failure possibilities, go for broke, damn the torpedoes' full steam ahead, put it all on the line, sink or swim, it ain't over till the fat lady sings, never say never, No guts no glory is my advice to a 3rd party.

To hell with being hemmed in look what it has gotten freedom loving Americans. We have two main political parties in the USA and the only major difference is speed. One party is rushing into full socialism at warp speed and the other is crawling with a drip, drip slow motion torture into full socialism.

Sure, the liberals with their nearly 50 percent hardcore government dependents are going to win for now. But, I'm going to stake my entire God given wisdom on the fact that the American people will never accept a political system that brings undue hardship, starving, and suffering.

Individual freedom is bred into the American people and I don't believe they are going to tolerate a system like in Europe. Socialism never has and never will work it only gets worse with time.

If a 3rd party make a stand the people will

come to them when they see socialism up close. That will especially be true if the two major parties keep growing government.

MR. SIRMANS' DEEP DARK SECRET THAT HE IS ABOUT TO EXPOSE?

Since I have been giving my strong opinion on a lot of things lately I decided to go whole hog all the way and make it a clean slate. Hell, it could be the smoking gun to some and finally confirm that I really am off my rocker.

I didn't have to do this; I could have forever kept this a deep dark secret and took it with me to my grave. Well, here goes my true belief on what I am about to admit to the whole wide world.

I would say I do believe to the tune of about 99.9 percent but I just can't bring myself to make it a complete 100 percent. "I don't believe that man has ever set foot on the moon."

Sure, I know the USA has orbited the moon with astronauts and broadcasted about landing and taking off from the moon. But, I believe the pictures were taken in the Nevada desert or somewhere like that. So, how do you like me now?

WRITERS OPINION:

Whoa, here! Let's keep our eye on the ball! Sometimes high decisions are made to placate possible lenders believing that no one wants to finance a gunslinger.

The USA has been reduced to a needy greedy financial dependent and I blame it all on our welfare state beast. It is impossible for the federal government to afford the cost of our welfare state but the liberals are in complete denial and out of touch with reality.

Nature's supreme law of "Natural selection" is now in the process of purging the whole system by letting the liberal anti-survival forces destroy almost everything. Then, out of the ruins will sprout forth a rebirth free of overpowering negative energy. But, what may rise up in a rebirth might not include individual freedom.

Otherwise, it is a long shot, but all the solutions can be found in reading Freddie L. Sirmans, Sr.'s books and writing's.
SIRMANS LOG: 7 APRIL 2010, 1429 HOURS.

WRITER'S OPINION:
When I see the liberals trying to sell the American people on the greatness of their super "Health care" victory it makes me think of a song I once heard.

Two women were competing for the same

23

man and afterward the winner realized her big, big prize was a snake oil salesman. So, she said something to this effect, "I thought I was the best of woman but was the biggest fool!"

So, before this health care debacle is over I believe a lot more people will realize that instead of being the wisest supporters they were the biggest fools.

WHY GREED CAN PREVENT MASS STARVING FROM STRIKING THE USA WITHIN 3 YEARS!!!

Misunderstanding "Greed" is the perfect example of liberals and uninformed people failing to understand human nature. It is impossible to create a wealthy nation without greed and self-interest being allowed to flourish.

Sure, like electricity greed is very dangerous and must be bridled, but it should never be shut down or restricted too severely if wealth is to be created in a nation. There is no greater or powerful energy packed motivating force in nature than greed.

That is why communism, socialism, and every non-free market place will always fail and face mass starvation unless the nation has vast natural resources to sell or receive outside help. A million things can be tried to

save the USA but I can guarantee you
nothing is going to save us unless one thing is
done first.

First, find people that will vote government
out of its super provider role or we all perish.
It is a power thing and big government as a
super provider is in a race right now to finish
consolidating it power for an absolute take
over.

Starting with the "New deal" the people have
surrendered almost all of their power to
control big government except the vote, and
its days are numbered, when we wake up
with no individual freedom it will be too late.
No one ever thought Germany would be
completely taken over either.

Whoever is the provider is the ruler and in a
showdown it may already be too late to
prevent a complete take over. I don't make
the rules I just have the wisdom to see what
is actually playing out. Even a fool should be
able to see what is taking place is not
business as usual.

That is why if government would just get the
hell out of the way and protect the country,
the free market place, and free competition,
then even the poorest of the poor could pay
for their own food and health care out of
pocket. But, oh no, then government couldn't
wield its God like power as a super sugar

daddy provider.

This is so simple and has been proven to work time and time again but liberals are too shallow to see past their noses. More and more I'm beginning to believe that the liberals gaining over whelming power was a blessing in disguise.

Otherwise, no amount of trying to convince people of the dangers of liberalism could have put the fear of God in the American people like this bunch has. Except for the nearly 40 percent hardcore dependents everyone else can hardly wait to vote this bunch out.

The pendulum could swing back the other way so hard it goes off the chart. I think they want to take over everything and make peons out of everybody. I believe they are going for the jugular to kill all individual freedom in the USA.

I think they want to bust the budget for a complete out right power grab through martial law.

WHO IS REALLY THE FOOL AND NUT CASE?

Over 95 percent of the American people think someone that thinks like me is a fool and nut case. I have the depth and wisdom that very few have and history will continue to prove me right. It can take a hundred years or longer, but there has never been and never will be a government that didn't go broke at some point.

History is littered with abandoned city ruins where all of the people left due to the economy collapsing. That is why I pound and pound so hard of the importance of culture, culture, and maintaining a strong nuclear and extended family system. It should be the responsibility of the nuclear and extended family to pay health care cost with or without insurance, not the government.

The same goes for keeping the homeless off the streets, not the government except as a last resort. What are the people going to do when the government is broke and don't have enough money to take care of the people? It is very simple; there is absolutely no way a nation can survive through hard times without a strong nuclear and extended family foundation.

Even worse in our case our welfare state beast has all but completely destroyed our culture, our nuclear and extended family system, and any capacity to barter. And this beast is protected by the liberals standing guard for it to finish the job of annihilating the USA.

The African American community is like the

canary in a mine, the two parent married family will soon be something you find only in the history books.

Any reasonable intelligent person knows this economy is headed for a collapse, but don't know what the solutions are, I do. However, the most dangerous things to the survival of the USA are government red tape and mandates.

Like in California the red tape keeps the people from saving themselves, no individual or group can use initiative to save themselves without the state taking almost all of the profit. No one wants to work for nothing.

Anything that belongs to everyone in practice belongs to no one. That is something liberals can't see. Bless their hearts, but, they should never be in charge of this nation's long term survival.

Yet, my plea for sanity is seen as this raving maniac right wing nut case that must be ignored. Sure, I agree, I'm a driven man, but it is for the survival of my country which I believe has lost its way. All of the solutions can be found in my vast writing and books.

THE ONLY THING MISSING NOW IS THE SECRET POLICE AND THE KNOCK IN THE MIDDLE OF THE NIGHT!!! AND THAT

WILL BE NEXT!!!
HEALTH CARE PASSING MAY COLLAPSE THE USA ECONOMY AND BRING DOWN GLOBAL ECONOMY WITH IT!!!

Liberals and shallow minded people thanks raising taxes brings in more income to the government, but in reality with few exceptions it proves just the opposite. After a point more taxes just changes behavior and brings in far less revenue and we are far past that point.

With all of the new taxes and tax hikes instead of the government taking in more revenue a year from now I predict the take will be much, much less, plus there will be many more mouths to feed along with many, many more bill to pay. Give me a break, spare me.

Only a weak survival instinct and poor judgment would allow this to happen and I blame it all on our welfare state. The liberals have taken this great nation into fantasy land while good men stood by and did nothing.

I may be wrong and have been wrong many times before, still, I predict within one year after this "Big vote" passes the USA economy will have collapsed or be on the brink. I am writing these words on the eave of the "Big vote" that will determine the survival of the industrial world as we know it.

I have the exceptional God given wisdom to know beyond a shadow of doubt that the USA economy will collapse and bring the global economy down with it. I know less than five percent of the American people have the depth and wisdom to believe anything I say; still, only history can prove me wrong.

All of the answers on how to save the USA and world economy can be found in reading my books and writings. These liberals mean well and truly believe they are right but they are blind and don't know it. In reality they don't understand human nature.

.

Understanding human nature is something that can't be taught, it can only be learned from real or imposed hardship and struggle. A human being is not just another cog in a machine, if you take away his struggle to survive you destroy his character and make him a useless dependent, but, you can never convince a liberal of that simple fact.

.

They think someone like me that will only help someone that will help themselves is cruel and uncaring. America is great because great men with great wisdom made it great, not shallow minded do gooders that think doing for someone is teaching them how to survive.

SIRMANS LOG: 20 MARCH 2010, 1156 HOURS.

THE "BIG VOTE" AFTER WORDS
The deed is done. These good men and women in congress truly believe they have done what is in the best interest of their country. Who truly knows the Lord works in mysterious ways? With all of my great wisdom and judgment I totally disagree with what they have done.

I felt the same way I did when I watched the government kill the innocent Terri Schiavo. I felt like a helpless soul powerless to stop a violent crime from taking place. However, we are a nation ruled by law instead of men and I respect the law as much as anyone.

Life will go on but it will not be the same, I know I won't be the same. I believe the laws of nature that works to keep balance in the universe will use divine intervention to save individual freedom.

I believe an individual or a movement will come about and save the last bastion of true freedom left in the world today. Or course I may be wrong, but, what the heck!!??!!!???

NOW ONLY THE SECOND AMENDMENT PROTECTS USA FREEDOM!!!

With this complete liberal takeover of health care in the USA that means they are going for the jugular of individual freedom in America. In almost no time all private insurance companies will be forced out of business.

All medical cost will double and you will be forced to pay or go to prison and loose everything you own. If that happens the only thing that stands between the complete lost of all individual freedom in the USA will be the second amendment, and its days will be numbered.

All of the answers that can save the USA with freedom still intact can be found in Freddie L. Sirmans, Sr's books and writings, take heed.

NOW CHEW ON THIS!!!
PREVIEW OF USA FUTURE IF LIBERALS GET THEIR WAY!!!
Today a non free market place economy cannot exist without most of its people starving half to death. That is contrary to what the anti-capitalist ingrates think.

In past history dictators and authoritarian governments would use their armies to make weaker countries supply them with food and resources, or starve most of their own people half to death. In this modern nuclear age bulling and taking over weaker countries and living off the spoils is not going to be tolerated.

No one works extra hard and produces when someone else is sitting on their ass and receiving an equal reward. In a non free market system like that everyone tries to do the least to eat and avoid being shot.

With Fannie and Freddie gobbling up all of the real estate and their boss the federal government gobbling up banks and the automobile industry it won't be long before we citizens will be just peons.

Here is something else you can chew on, whoever are the provider rules and it sure ain't the American people anymore like it was before the "New deal."

Unless a way is found to vote the federal government out of its super sugar daddy provider role it is only a matter of time before a dictator seizes power.

However, the American voters still has the power and must stop this now because practically all politicians loves the God like power that comes with being a super sugar daddy provider and will not yield one inch.

It may already be too late with so many needy government dependents.

THE REAL REASON JOBS WENT OVERSEAS!!!

A lot of people wonder and can't understand why would our politicians send our jobs overseas? At one time they were actually subsidizing and encouraging companies to move out of the country. These are not bad people they mean well like all liberals.

Since the "New deal" liberals from both political parties have tax fed a welfare state baby into what we have now a full grown welfare state beast. And many will sell their soul, their country, and whatever they can get their hands on to keep feeding this welfare state beast.

It is very simple the liberals sent our jobs overseas in order to keep feeding our welfare state beast. Even back in the 1980's the increasing tax bite on big business was more than they could carry and stay in business, otherwise the USA economy would have collapsed in the early 1990's.

So, in order to keep feeding the welfare state beast they knew big business must have a way to cut expenses. Politicians decided cheap labor was the way to help big business keep generating the tax money to keep their welfare state beast fed. That same thinking is what created globalization, which in my view is a fool's game.

So they greased the fast track and off went our jobs out of the country. This liberal created welfare state beast has corrupted us all too some degree how else would we keep voting the same big spenders back into office. Lord have mercy.

Why demagogue the insurance companies, they don't have a gun to anyone's head making them buy, if they don't make a profit they don't survive.

When this welfare state beast forces all insurance companies out of business you are going to prison or lose everything you own if don't pay a lot more than you are paying now. Government operate on power not market forces, you'll find out!!!

ECONOMISTS CAN'T SAVE USA FROM DOOM!!!

Perspective is the reason why my great wisdom is superior to most. I see the one leg economy in relationship to the three other legs of the four legged survival stool.

Whereas, the tunnel vision of most economists is guided by facts and figures as far as the eye can see. "Natural selection (the invisible hand)" controls an economy, in time facts and figures will always fail. The other three legs to the survival stool can be found in reading Freddie L. Sirmans' books and writings.

I am speaking with divine supernatural
wisdom when I say the only way I see to
save the USA as one nation with individual
freedom still intact is to first abolish the
minimum wage. Next, abolish almost all taxes
on businesses and everything else except a
very small property tax.

Third, kick the government out of its provider
role by privatizing damn near everything and
setup mass emergency public kitchens,
shelters, and clinics, and then I'll guarantee
you entrepreneurs and the free market will
save this great nation intact. Of course this
won't happen or even be considered.

Power always goes down with the ship and is
going to take all of us down, too. Throughout
history there has never been a nation that
changed course knowingly headed for a
crash. It may not be the type of rope it wants
but at least I have thrown the nation a life
line.

I know almost everyone is thinking, "Oh my
God," the government needs more money not
less to take care of more and more people.
Wrong, that is the mentality that got this
great nation in this mess.

If we could just get the government out of
the free market place and its provider role it

would automatically guarantee our survival, but, I'm just one lone writer ranting and raving before deaf ears, how sad.

<u>SANTA CLAUS AND THE TOOTH FAIRY!!!</u>
People are being told that the economy is going to recover, well, in my opinion that is like believing in Santa Claus and the tooth fairy. All government income is taken out of the profit margins of some kind of businesses or business transaction and in more and more cases not leaving enough profit for the business to survive.

No business can exist without making a profit. Every day local, state, and the federal government is taking in less and less revenue due to business failures that is because of too high taxes, fees, permits, license costs, and on and on.

Instead of the government decreasing taxes and cutting spending it is doing just the opposite by hiring thousands of new employees and increasing spending by the trillions. It is not possible to get blood out of a turnip, but it seems the federal government is trying to do just that. God, I ask in your name save this great land of the free.

Come on folks, why crucify the man for letting his kids talk on the air traffic control radio. What's done is done, why take away the man's livelihood. What really need to be done is ban all kids from air traffic control towers, period. Only liberals and shallow minded people that can't take a joke would treat an innocent lack of good judgment like a murder case.

Just as Hoover couldn't stand in the way of a baby welfare state, there was absolutely no way Bunning could continue standing in the way of this full grown super welfare state beast. We are doomed!!!

All government income originates from some form of private sector excess profit, period. There are no ifs, ands, or buts about that fact. Keeping this welfare state beast fed is the cause for us eating our seed corn and still we won't kill this beast and free ourselves.

Not only that, it has almost destroyed any means for the USA to remain a civilized nation. It has almost destroyed our nuclear and extended family system, our moral and family values (homosexual porn can't be avoided), and any emergency bartering capacity for economical survival.

And only now a few people seem to be gravely concern, mainstream media is still out to lunch. All of the answers and solutions can be found in Freddie L. Sirmans books and writing.

And another thing, true individual freedom is about common sense and thinking for yourself. Be aware, there are many false prophets today with the gift of gab that can be super charming and extremely mesmerizing with a new twist.

Cock and bull conspiracy theories are a dime a dozen, as long as one never forget to do the thinking and deciding for themselves. Freedom also means deciding if I, Freddie L. Sirmans, Sr. with all of my free advice am some type of snake oil salesman myself, I think not, you decide.

A strong nuclear and extended family system is responsible for paying for those that can't pay their own medical cost. Insurance companies don't have a gun to any one's head making them buy.

The only thing the federal government should be responsible for is paying for national defense, administrative, and a few interior cost, period; anything else is against the constitution.

Overwhelmingly the thinking is all wrong in this great country; we have lost our way and are chasing a rainbow. There is no pot of gold at the end of the rainbow, only heart ache and pain.

I think it's around 25,000 homes mortgages lost every day in the USA. Well, that tallies up to a lot of people not paying property taxes and is a big loss of revenue for local governments.

Sometimes I feel my writing is not getting traction, then I axe myself what is the alternative, to give up on saving freedom in America, me, never.

THE BIG LIE!!!
I'm so sick and tired of hearing this big lie that the bail out money avoided a depression in the USA. Hog wash, poppycock, Bull crap, or whatever, there ain't gonna be a depression in the USA because we no longer have the culture or the infrastructure to support a depression.

With the course we are on it is no longer a matter of a collapse, it's now when will it hit. With no emergency backup bartering capacity we will zip right pass a depression stage to the next stage, total chaos or some type of authoritarian rule.

All of the remedies and solutions to save the USA are found in my books and writing. You avoid a depression by getting the government the hell out of private enterprise and its super sugar daddy provider role, period.

THE USA IS DIGGING ITS OWN GRAVE!!!
A nation's long term survival depends on maintaining and safe-guarding a strong culture. A strong culture means having a strong nuclear and extended family system, a strong family and moral code in place, and a minimum bartering capacity.

Money as a currency is vastly more efficient than bartering, still paper money is supposed to represent a physical currency backup, and a physical currency backup is supposed to represent goods and services.

The physical currency backup link has been compromised thereby allowing a false economy to thrive. And the price for that has been the destruction of our culture and any backup capacity to barter, which is insane. Culture and bartering is civilization, you can't have one without the other.

Civilization and bartering existed long before money or a currency was invented. A nation with a strong culture and emergency backup bartering capacity can survive without money, but no amount of money can save a nation with a weak culture and no emergency backup bartering capacity.

Our welfare state beast is about to finish off

destroying what's left of our culture and less than minimum bartering capacity. There are simply not enough people in the USA growing and raising their own food, and the price we are going to pay is mass starvation sooner than we think.

A nation can't have adequate emergency backup bartering capacity unless enough people have their own food to barter with. We can't keep having our cake and eating it too. There is no foreign enemy spending this country into oblivion, it is people "We" ourselves are voting into office.

MY PHILOSOPHY ON ECONOMICS by Freddie L. Sirmans, Sr.

If I have to repeat it 10,000 times, "Natural selection" is what controls economics. Just like it is as equal important to be able to forget thing as it is to remember things except we never realizes it. The same applies to economics, it is just as important to have purges or busts as it is to have booms, you can't have one without the other.

The secret to everything in life is balance, even good and evil. How else is Mother Nature going to control moral decay, gross inefficiency, and over powering corruption without collapses and rebirths? Leaders of old knew this wisdom. Now, far too many people believe that big government should come in and prevent all failure, a very big mistake.

That closes off all safety valves to the system itself and allows the negative and anti survival forces to survive and become more and more powerful until they bring down the whole system. You can't have an economy without booms and busts, it is a life cycle the way nature designed it.

Man's responsibility is to safeguard and keep a strong enough culture to survive and get through rebirths or busts whenever they occur. When small rebirths or busts occur, no problem, the problem is when the small rebirth safety valves are shut off by preventing failures like we have done, now the whole system is about to blow.

Mr. Sirmans with his great wisdom has laid out the solutions and remedies in his books and writing.

IS A FINANCIAL COLLAPSE IMMINENT?

This thing about an economic recovery and creating all kinds of make-work jobs, well, my great wisdom tells me a recovery ain't gonna happen and make-work jobs is going to hasten the collapse.

Remember, our welfare state beast feeds on more-money and every job loss means more mouths to feed with less and less tax money coming into the till.

Under this circumstance a collapse is imminent unless the federal government jettisons its super heavy social and family financial load by weaning or privatizing out of it.

It is impossible for the federal government to continue to carry this heavy financial load without collapsing. This is the belief of one lone writer, me, Freddie L. Sirmans, Sr.. I have no power to make anyone see the light.

I know I will continue to be written off as some kind of extremist right wing nut case, so be it, I mean well with good intentions. With love always.

THE PARTY OF "NO" LABEL!!!
I think the party of "No" label is a badge of honor. The liberals are caught out in the open with no one on hand to blame and hide behind.

They know the only thing that can save their hide in the 2010 election is to do what they do best, find a way to shift blame to someone else.

So, "Be aware of all Greeks bearing gifts." The tax paying voters love hearing the word "No" and is going to prove it in the 2010 election if anyone is still saying "No."

WRITER FINALLY LOSES IT!?!?
Maybe I have lost it, like the paranoid fellow that thought when the football players went into a huddle they were talking about him.

Well, for some reason when they make these "Bed wetting" remarks I keep thinking they are talking about me.

No, no, snap out of it Freddie, that's not possible. However, maybe this time I really have lost it.

GOD SAVE US FROM OUR BELOVED EDUCATED FOOLS!!!
After the latest supreme court decision in favor of free speech for all I am in shock by the liberal reaction. My God! I didn't know how deep the hatred of big business and free enterprise had become in this great country.

I ask where is all this flawed ignorant thinking coming from. I suspect it must be coming from our college and university systems. I thank God for our corporations, without them the USA would be worse off than most third world countries. The true problem in the USA is big government and the welfare state not big business.

Big business can't survive if it doesn't make a profit. How can you attack corporations and at the same time complain about lack of jobs if you are not ignorant. Jobs don't just drop out of heaven, who the hell do they think provide jobs if not corporations, give me a break.

I see people on TV talking about creating jobs that don't have a clue as to where jobs come from. Jobs are based on supply and demand to make a profit. Only government can create make-work jobs with you and me paying for them.

With federal, state, and local governments all taking their growing tax bite first its extremely hard for any business to make enough profit to survive let alone create more jobs. Not to mention all kinds of the license fees, permit fees, different sale taxes, and other governments mandates imposed on a business.

The fact is we have a social and family provider welfare state and there is not enough money in the whole wide world to keep feeding this beast. And we have a leadership in complete denial that won't condition the people to plant and relearn to survive like our forefathers. God save us from our beloved educated fools.

Corporations we need and love you, the

common people throughout the USA like in
Massachusetts are fed up.

USA LIFE BOAT!?!?!

As a writer with supernatural wisdom the only
way I see to save the USA federal
government is through less financial
obligations, but, from arrogance it is still
taking on more financial obligations, which is
insane and anti survival.

To save all of the USA as one nation, wisdom
dictates that we first save the federal
government at all cost otherwise the USA
splits into many pieces. When so much
depends on government to survive the
government can't just walk away, but, to fail
to wean out of it is weak and irresponsible.

Here is the remedy as I see it, the federal
government must jettison damn near all
social and provider obligations through
privatization, get rid of the minimum wage,
and cut all taxes to the bone. Then the
federal government will have a fighting
chance to survive, otherwise only doom lies
ahead.

To ignore this deep wisdom advice is to tempt
fate and USA survival as one nation. That is
the way it is, this ship is sinking and the
federal government better take a life boat
soon or go down with the ship.

THE HAITI DEBACLE?!?!
HAITI

As a creative original thinker I've tried very hard not to comment on Haiti because I pull no punches and tell it as I see it. But, I couldn't take it any longer I was about to pop I had to vent.

No one believes in freedom and democracy more than I do, however, there is no one thing in life that will work for every case. I seen it on TV and remember several years ago Haiti was fairly well run by their military.

The place had law and order and was a safe place for foreign investments. Several foreign factories had located there with more to come. However, there was a problem, there were reports of citizens being abused and mistreated.

Whoa, hell no, said the big giant to the north we can't have that, we must restore democracy to this sovereign state. Their military was given the boot and sent packing. Now, Haiti has been turned into a failed welfare state like the liberals has done to Michigan and are trying to do to the entire USA.

Haiti is a microcosm of what's coming to the USA if the death grip the liberals have on our great country is not broken soon. The exception being Haiti has never been a democracy and probably never will be a democracy. And in my opinion the same applies to Iraq.

PS: All of that aside now is the time to donate; I have already donated $50.00 and will be giving more than and as much as my budget can stand.

* February 03, 2010 donated $25.00
* March 02, 2010 donated $25.00

"IT IS ALL OUT IN THE OPEN NOW, NOTHING ELSE TO HIDE" Right after the last election that swept in a new liberal president and super liberal majorities in both houses of congress, I said these words "It is all out in the open now, liberals will have no one else to blame, and all eyes will be on them alone."

Around eight months later after all of the "Tea Party" hype I said if voters get fed up and decide to change political horses, all you will get is a slower political team into full socialism. I still stand by that. So, to the political team now on the sideline, just hold your horses, you will be swept in in the next two elections.

Then what are you going to do? Are you

going to be just a slower team into full socialism like in the past, or are you going to take down this welfare state beast set on enslaving this great predominant Christian nation, otherwise" Lead, follow, or get the hell out of the way" a third party movement will be unstoppable.

FED UP AND DISGUSTED, I SLAM MY HAT ON THE FLOOR I don't care who you are if you tell me health care should be free you are ignorant, a moron, and don't understand freedom or democracy.

With your thinking that health care should be free then food, clothing, and housing should be free too there is no difference. If you have a gripe about the price, me too, the price is past the sky is the limit and somewhere out in space due to the government getting into health care in the first place.

The only way health care could be free is if the doctors, nurses, and other health care provider became slaves and cared for you free of charge. Joking aside, saying it should be free, I know that means the government should pay for it.

The people that believe that don't have a clue as to where government income actually comes from. Like a little kid believes eggs come only from the grocery store, ninety five percent of the American people believe government income comes only from the tax payers.

Most of the money from individual tax payers and business tax payers comes out of the profit margin of the barely hanging on small business men and women of America. So, with the government demanding more and more of small business's profit, soon there won't be any successful businesses left, because no business can hire or survive unless it makes a profit.

No profit means no businesses or paid employees for the government to tax. Then all of the millions upon millions of do-for-me government dependents our liberal welfare state beast has produced will be rioting in the streets and at each others throats.

BRIEF BACK TO THE STONE AGE LECTURE
Through out my writing I have mention civilization going back to the Stone Age and for that a lot of people think I'm crazy and ignorant.

That is because so few understand basic economics. Basic economics starts with the individual nuclear and extended family system then leads on to a community bartering system.

However, bartering is an extremely limited economic system because no one may want what you have to offer and then you are stuck. Gold, silver, or some other rare precious metal used as a currency solved the extremely limited bartering problem.

Still, the value of a physical currency is in the currency itself no matter who has it. A government can't manipulate and devalue a physical currency when the value is in the currency itself, or print up and handout money it don't have.

Fast forward to today, the welfare state with its unlimited capacity to tax and print worthless paper money has almost destroyed our nuclear and extended family system along with any capacity to barter. And without these basic foundation building blocks no society can survive through hard times, it is impossible.

Folks, I will sum up by saying, I'm just a lone writer doing my thing, and telling it as I see it. I have a fifty fifty or one out of two chance of being right. Besides, who listens to me, a whole lot of people think I'm a kook and off my rocker anyway.

There really is no guaranteed individual wealth anymore. If you bury or hide money under the mattress today next week there may be a whole new world currency. Also, no individual truly owns property anymore with the cost of property taxes and it may be twice as much next year.

Get a grip people; you better use your vote sensible and vote out these big progressive liberal spenders while you still can. Love you, and thanks for reading my work, God bless.

THE BIG TRIAL IN NEW YORK CITY.

Let me throw my two cent worth in here. In my mind there is no limit to how shallow liberals can be. Protect New York City from what! Sure the trial is going to go on and definitely will be protected.

But, it is the roll of the dice and is opening up a can of worms. Can New York City protect every store, hotel, mall, rail road, and on and on like in Tel Aviv. Why invite the unknown, lets just hope my extreme caution is just pesky nonsense.

MINIMUM WAGE:

A minimum wage is like a vehicle with no reverse or an army walled of from any retreat. Getting rid of the minimum wage and cutting taxes to the bone will at least save the USA from total chaos and allow us to live and fight another day.

Where do most citizen tax payers get their

money, from their small business employers? Where do businesses get their money, from citizen customers, some of which they themselves employ. As you can see the economy operates as a giant cycle.

Human energy and intelligence creating something of value in the form of food and resources is what keeps this cycle going. And the rewarding byproduct of the whole process is what's called profit. That is what government takes, all taxes ultimately comes from some form of profit.

Sure, government needs a certain amount of profit driven tax money to protect the nation from both foreign and domestic enemies and basic interior needs. But, the USA government was never designed to be a cradle to grave social and family provider.

Now, big government at all levels is taking far too much of small businesses profit for many of them to survive let alone hire anyone. And you gonna tell me mass tax cuts to the bone is not the answer, go fly a kite!!!

STONE AGE:
Most people with common sense think the biggest threat to the survival of the USA is its financial crisis cause by big government spending. I don't think so, I think what is slowly driving the dagger in the

heart of this great nation is what big government has done to our nuclear and extended family system.

No famine, financial collapse, nuclear attack, mass chemical attack, or mass biological attack can destroy this huge nation with our strong nuclear and extended family system along with our minimum bartering capacity is this statement true or false? Then you be the judge.

In terms of raw survival big government as the welfare state has destroyed everything and left us with a leadership in complete denial along with countless gimmy, gimmy, do for me dependents. Culture and survival wise just about the only option we have left is to regress back to the Stone Age unless our leaders snap out of denial and face cold steel rock hard reality.

Folks, I'm just a lowly lone writer telling it as I see it, pray that I'm wrong. Like a broken record I repeat, no one wants this but it would keep us from going back to the Stone Age. Get rid of the minimum WAGE and cut taxes to the bone across the board.

Then whatever income the government takes in should first go to national defense and administrative cost, and whatever is left go to community kitchens, hospitals, and shelters. Sure, its extreme but it is better than going back to the Stone Age. If anyone has a better solution they better step up now because I see the Stone Age over the horizon.

Everybody is all worked up over health care and socialism. But, unless my advice to get rid of the minimum wage and cut taxes to the bone is taken serious nothing is going to stop the USA and global economy from going back to the Stone Age.

Cost, cost, and more cost is the problem with health care and if the government thinks it can take it over and not pay the cost it will destroy medical care in America. However, it is going to take it over anyway if not today it will be tomorrow, because the only way to stop it would be to dismantle the welfare state and I'll leave it at that.

And the root reason why medical cost has shot through the roof pass the sky is the limit into outer space is because government got into it in the first place. Anything the government gets into in a free country the cost will always go through the roof because government doesn't adhere to market force principals. Enough said.

As to capitalism versus socialism that is the least of our problems. No form of government can save a nation from doom if it looses its nuclear and extended family foundation, which we have. I know I keep writing the same thing over and over but if I can enlighten just one mover and shaker it will be worth it. Amen.

* Scroll down to read recovery BULL...
This is when one desperately needs to stay awake because life, property, or job may be on the line.

Technique: Hold any small object such as a quarter, house keys, car keys, etc. in your hand, if you start to doze off it will drop and when it hits the floor you will snap awake every time, just don't forget to pick it up. *This technique is not design for anyone driving a vehicle.

IS IT DESTINY OR FROM A HIGHER POWER?

I, Freddie L. Sirmans, Sr. a shy neurotic uneducated south Georgia USA country boy is now teaching the world basic economics, somebody need to teach it. Ninety nine percent of the American people don't know what is actually powering this big USA and global economic ship.

Without this source power the whole USA and global economy will be left adrift. Almost everyone thinks its power comes from the government and the American tax payers. That is a source but it is not the root source, plus almost all thinking stops there.

Very few probe deeper and discovers who is actually paying taxes to the government. And even those that do acknowledge that it is the business and working people of America, and that is the end of it.

American small businesses do employ far more people in this country than anything else so that must be the main source powering the USA economy. Well, I guess that's it we have an open and shut case.

Whoa, not so fast, I beg the difference, for the record I will prove that it is something called "Profit" that is the root source that powers the USA economy or any successful economy. We all need a certain amount of food and basic resources to live on. So, whatever amount over what we need to survive on is what's called extra or profit that we can exchange for money or whatever.

The accumulation of excess profit is what makes one rich or wealthy. A business is only a medium to exchange goods or services for a profit, no profit, no business, no employee, and nothing for the government to tax. Big government at all levels, federal, state, and local has put so many taxes, license fees, permit fees, rules, regulations, and other mandates on a business that it is a miracle anyone makes a profit.

Almost any blood sucking economic system will work for 80-100 years, then its hell to pay. This welfare state system is like a dog chasing its tail because a business is only a means of exchange; all cost must be passed on to the public which in turn raises the cost of living on everyone. I rest my case your honor.

The USA economy is now at the point it fits the old proverbial saying: "A straw broke the camels back."

LATE ENTRY II:

I once heard this story about a man with a mule that would walk about twenty yards or so stop briefly and continue on and on. Someone asked the owner what was the problem with this mule, why he acted like that?

The owner said the mule was afraid he might not hear the owners command so he stops to listen. Well, I think that same analogy can be applied to the liberals running this country.

They have all of the power and are almost totally in control of this great country. So, what is the problem with them, why are they acting the way they are? I ask why don't they just follow their own beliefs and convictions and stop all of this stopping for bipartisan support.

The fact is: The idea of taking on responsibility all alone with no one else on hand to shift blame to, scares the hell out of a liberal.

LATE ENTRY:
The financial burden load of the welfare state has bankrupted this nation and sent our manufacturing and jobs over seas. But, that is not the worst thing the welfare state beast has done to this great predominate Christian nation.

The worst thing is it has ripped out the inner fabric of this great nation by destroying our nuclear and extended family system, and any capacity to barter, there is no recovery from this, and Stone Age here we come. However, the future is never written in stone. Getting rid of the minimum wage and cutting taxes to the bone can still save us.

Getting rid of the minimum wage and cutting taxes to the bone, you must be crazy, of course that's not going to happen, and the power structure and big money will go down in flames first. If only enough common sense citizens would pledge to vote for people willing to get rid of the minimum wage and cut taxes to the bone this great predominate Christian nation would be saved.

* There is an old saying that: "If you say something long enough and loud enough eventually someone is going to believe you." Maybe not mine but some nation is going to believe me.

Okay, everybody knows the moon effects crime and the ebb and flow of the tides. Brace yourself, the moon is about to strike back, pun intended, he, he, he...

Draft fear and the liberal media was really what caused the lost in Vietnam. Even General Giap himself admitted something to that of fact when he said only the America media gave them the hope to fight on.

With bombing accuracy and other high technology US military advantages are ten times greater than back then.

"Quitters don't win and winners don't quit." Just an opinion by writer, Freddie L. Sirmans, Sr.

RECOVERY, RECOVERY, BS!
My God! My God! Come on folks, economics ain't rocket science; a hundred and fifty years ago almost everyone knew what I keep telling people. It is not just the shallow minded

61

liberals, hardly anyone anymore have a strong survival instinct.

Anyone that thinks the USA can continue to carry the financial burdens of our big government welfare state is either in complete denial or just plain ignorant. If you think I am a fool and nut case, you are wrong.

History has proven that it is always the masses that are wrong. I have the wisdom and survival instinct to know beyond a shadow of a doubt that I'm right, so help me God. However, reason never changes closed minds.

Very few people truly understand how an economy works as well as I do. Almost everyone think in term of big money, but it is not the amount it is the buying power that counts in the long run.

The other team can't run up the score if you got the ball. It is the same in economically terms; prices can't go above what the always larger poorer population can afford to pay. That is unless a big government welfare state unconstitutionally hands out free money on an individual basis.

That act subsidizes high prices, and is what feeds this never ending inflationary spiral that we are caught up in. Sure, you can help the poor, but you can't hand out cash and food stamps on an individual basis and not destroy the free market place price structure.

That is because there is just two teams the seller (merchants) and the Buyer (consumers). And the government is supposed to fill the role of referee and tax collector. However, that is no longer the case the government is taking tax money from one team and giving it to the other.

Mother Nature says hell no, that breaks nature's supreme law of "Natural selection;" and she is preparing to step in and create a rebirth by starving the whole system back to the Stone Age.

If the government was not hogging the free market place, the free market place would heal itself. Now, the only way to get this beast out of the market place is to starve it out, it has grown far too powerful. Otherwise, there is no way to keep the USA from starving to death in just a very few years, you mark my word.

In my view the USA and the global economy is in a state of mass denial. No one wants to face the cold steel rock hard reality. If I have to repeat it a thousand times, man cannot use figures and intelligence to manage a successful economy because the variables are infinite.

However, there is nothing complicated or secret about how to run a time tested successful economy. There is a proven time tested ideology that has never failed to produce far more food and goods than any one nation can consume.

That ideology is, "Allow free competition and let the free market work," it is just that simple. But no, today we have all of these learned economists that think they can out smart Mother Nature, wrong. It is like having a vehicle with no reverse, you can't have a free floating free market place economy with a minimum wage.

You can't have a lasting free market place economy when sky high taxes and every other kind of government mandate is siphoning off most of a business's profit. For a democracy to survive and last every individual and family unit must carry its own weight. I keep hearing about a recovery, that is BULLSHIT!

I can only speak for my self, but in my view it is impossible to have a recovery with all of the financial burdens our welfare state is now carrying, after years of adding more and more the load is just too much. Also, I believe unless the minimum wage is junked and taxes cut to the bone more and more businesses are going to fail with even higher unemployment.

Listen up! Profit, profit, profit, is everything; there will be nothing for the government to survive on itself if not enough business's is making enough profit to stay afloat.

The government can only tax a profitable business, no one making a profit, nothing for the government to tax because not even Joe public gets paid if he doesn't have a job, it's just that simple. Think about it.

According to the constitution the only financial burdens our federal government should be carrying is to protect the nation from foreign and domestic enemies and to finance a healthy interior department.

But, oh no, we gave the "New deal" a foot in the door and since then liberal politicians from both parties have created this welfare state beast that is determine to grab absolute power and take away our individual freedom.

I say hell no! This beast has taken on financial burdens galore even as small as a hangnail, all out of the hard earned profits of the barely hanging on large and small business men/women of America. I say, snap out of it learned economists, face reality; lets take our bitter medicine and go boldly into the future.

We can do all things through God which strengthens us, Phil. 4-13 paraphrased.

UNDERSTANDING INFLATION!

In my view there is a big difference between the excessive printing of money inflation and the true cost of living inflation. I don't think very many people including economists understand what causes and drives true cost of living inflation, I do, and nuggets of it is found throughout my writing.

Printing a lot of worthless money alone can't drive the cost of living up. Government spending alone can't drive the cost of living up. Government can spend and build like crazy and that alone still won't drive the cost of living up.

There is only one way to drive the cost of living up on everyone, government consumer price support, there is simply no other way it can be done that I can see. An economy consists of only two players, the merchant and the consumer.

The process of "Natural selection" will always maintain a natural balance between the two. That is what controls and runs every economy. Sure, man can tinker and fiddler around with it but sooner or later the process of "Natural select" is going to complete a rebirth cycle. And the smartest thing man can do is maintain and safeguard a strong enough culture to survive a collapse or rebirth.

When the government gives masses of people on an individual basis enough money to pay whatever the merchant demands that is what drives inflation. Every penny the government takes comes out of the profit margin of some business or service if traced back far enough.

So, the more government takes the higher price the business will have to charge consumers to make a profit, or go out of business. That is what sets up the cost of living inflationary spiral that forces government to keep raising taxes higher and higher to give its masses of dependents enough money to support higher and higher merchant prices in a never ending spiral.

The truth of the whole matter is I can't see how the USA economy can last very much longer as a social and family provider. I can only hopes and pray for a miracle because that is what it is going to take to save the USA as one nation.

TEA PARTIES AND TOWN HALL MEETINGS ARE A WASTE OF TIME.

I don't enjoy raining on anyone's parade; I'm just writing what I think and believe, please forgive me. In my view the tea parties and town hall meetings is a lot of ado but lacking in problem solving. The first question I ask is what do anyone involved expect to result after all of the effort.

If someone can give me just one problem that will be solved after all of the effort I will gladly eat crow and backpedal. What is the focus? You can't solve a problem if you don't focus on it. When a predator goes after a prey meal he/she doesn't go after the whole herd, no, just one is focused upon, otherwise it is wasted effort.

Let's just say that after all of the tea party excitement is over, the voting public throws one political party out and change horses. All you will get is a slower team. The welfare state beast will still be consolidating more and more power for the eventually take over. However, I am so proud of the decent caring Americans trying to take back their country; maybe I am wrong on this. I hope so.

The only way I see our individual freedom is going to be saved is for the people and the states to take back control over the federal government. And that can only be done by starving this beast out of its all powerful social and family provider role, which the American voters are not prepared to do. We might as well accept our sad fate. I know deep in my heart that only a miracle can save the last great bastion of true freedom in the world today.

My take is the welfare state beast is biding its time. It knows it is firmly in control as the great super family provider with millions upon millions of dependents that is not going to bite the hand that feeds them. However, the American voting public still has the power to take back control of the federal government for themselves but don't know how.

Even worse the voting public doesn't have the will to take back control even if they did know how. That said, I will tell you how to take back control of your government. Focus on voting in office only people that is willing to "get rid of the minimum wage and cut taxes to the bone."

That is the only way to stop the welfare state beast from carrying out a complete take over of the USA. It is either the beast or us freedom loving Americans, there is no middle ground. If the American people are not willing to take down this beast by starving it out of its super family provider role, then no amount of tea parting or anything else is going to save individual freedom in America.

The founding fathers creation has been flipped upside down. Now, the federal government is the boss and has the power, and we the people and the states are almost powerless dependents that only have the vote. And the states don't even have 2 votes anymore because senators are no longer appointed by state legislatures.

And, we the people won't have the vote much longer unless we vote in people that will junk the minimum wage and cut taxes to the bone. That will starve this beast out of its all powerful family provider role. This nation was designed for the power to reside with the people and the states with the federal government filling the dependency role. I rest my case your honor.

Note: The USA junking the minimum wage and cutting taxes to the bone may put a stop to the spread of nuclear weapons as a byproduct, just a passing thought.

PS: Most people think I don't care about the desires and needs of the people, wrong. Sure, I care deeply, but my focus is so much, much bigger, it is about the sheer survival of my homeland as one nation with individual freedom still intact.

Most people don't believe the dire threats I keep talking about even exist. But, I have been blessed with the wisdom to know that it is real. I have already stated the only solution. Thank you God for my life health and strength. Amen.

IS A PERPETUAL MOTION ENGINE POSSIBLE?

The idea of a perpetual motion engine has been around probably as long as engines been around. Inventors have used compressed air, battery power, and anything you can think of trying to keep an engine running almost forever.

All for naught, the idea is an illusion. But, there are still people around today that think it's possible. It is the same way with an economy. There are still far too many people around today that think you can forever run an economy without a rebirth.

The facts are the same, it is all an illusion, and it can't be done. In economic survival terms stocks, bonds, and everything done on Wall Street is an illusion and side issue. No portfolio means anything if money has no value.

And even if money has value it means nothing if you have no food to eat or if those that have food won't sell. As I have said many times in terms of raw survival money are way down the list, people survived long before money was invented. In terms of long time survival culture is far more important than money.

No amount of money can save a nation when everyone is at each others throat. If the USA culture was strong and healthy far more people would agree with me and realize the only way to save the USA is to junk the minimum wage and cut taxes to the bone.

I can only hope I'm wrong, because I believe when we starts starving in mass numbers it will be because no one can start small and grow. It will be because the minimum wage and sky high taxes won't let entrepreneurs feed themselves and the nation.

Rich people are not the same as poor people with money, there is a world of difference in motivation and mentality. Lottery winners have proven that fact. When have any lottery winner ever built a financial empire that employed a hundred thousand people.

Socialism and communism fails because there are no entrepreneurs. And there are no entrepreneurs because there is no extra reward given for extra effort. Everybody tries to give the least amount of effort to survive.

No one in America have ever had to live in a system like that, we all need to be counting our blessings. Sure, everyone will be equal, but equal poor. I say, hell no!

THE LAST USA LIFELINE, TAKE IT!!!
If the USA is to survive two things must be done now, otherwise I, Freddie L. Sirmans,

Sr. can't see this great country surviving as one. Huh, who the hell are you, whoa, hold your horses, I'm just one lonely writer exercising my right of free speech while I still can, I don't expect to be taken seriously.

But, I am as deadly serious as a heart attack. The two must things: Junk the minimum wage and cut taxes to the bone immediately. The variables are just too numerous ONLY WHAT I JUST SAID WILL SAVE US from chaos and the total breakdown of western civilization, maybe even back to the stone age.

What happen to living off the land? Actually food and water can be free it is the piping and shipping that cost. High taxes and the minimum wage are going to be the bane that starves western civilization back to the Stone Age. It is better to work only for food and eat than it is to starve to death, in time a minimum wage places starving above eating.

You mark my word, very soon when this global economy starts unraveling there won't be anything left to do but starve because no one will be able to start small. Blocking almost all initiative will be the minimum wage and sky high taxes causing millions upon millions to starve NEEDLESSLY.

ONLY A MIRACLE CAN SAVE THE USA AS

ONE NATION.

I truly believe that only a miracle can save the USA as one nation. However, I do believe in miracles. It is sad for me to say but I believe it is only a matter of time before the liberals actually get their long awaited one payer medical care system. That doesn't mean anti big government opponents like me should just roll over.

When I look at the big battle going on, on capital hill about overhauling our medical care system it is no secret that the liberal's ultimate goal is socialized medicine. In my view its not going to matter a whole lot what they do because runaway medical cost can't be fixed until first the economy is fixed. And our economy can't be fixed until our welfare state beast is starved out of existence.

Yes, I said it, we must get rid of our welfare state, but I doubt you can find even 5 percent of the USA population that will agree with me on doing that. If you go back over 5 thousand years of written history there has never been any form of government like a welfare state until the "New Deal" came along.

The nuclear and extended family, the church, and social organizations have always taken care of the poor, homeless, and downtrodden, but never a government until western civilization followed the "New Deal" suit. Wise men of old had the wisdom to realize no matter what happens, don't ever destroy your lifeblood nuclear and extended family system by removing a survival need for it.

That is the one thing no civilization can recover from, that is why I cry and plead so hard for even an ounce of sanity. And I have over 5 thousand years of proof backing me up. The nuclear and extended family is the support and building block foundation of every society known to man, there are no exceptions.

Cutting taxes to the bone thereby creating a survival need for it is the only way to bring back the strong nuclear and extended family system that will save this great land of the free and home of the brave. Our welfare state is a provider form of government and that alone makes it the boss, dependents, you best mind your manners.

Like the saying goes, you can't have two captains of the same ship and sooner or later individual freedom is not going to survive with government as a social and family provider. It is already beginning to happen. Today the welfare state has created too many dependents that believe only in bigger and more government, so, now it is only a matter of when, not will the economy collapse.

I don't like admitting it, but the odds are in

favor of the liberals eventually getting everything they want, thereby destroying the USA for good in the process. The "New Deal and its programs allowed the camel to get it's nose under the tent, then flamboyant liberals using The gift of gab and The course of least resistant" sunk this country to where it is today.

Nature's law of "Taking the course of least resistance" affects us all too some degree and there is no getting around that fact. And the liberals are experts at "Taking the course of least resistance" and shifting blame, which in most cases is not the wisest course to take. The welfare state beast we have today is the result of mostly liberal thinking and spending money we don't have.

There is no doubt in my mind that individual freedom in the USA will not survive as long as our welfare state is in power. Nothing and I mean nothing is going to prevent it from eventually consolidating to absolute take over power, unless its money supply power source is taken away. That means this beast must be starved to death if individual freedom is to survive in the USA.

There is no other way; it is now either it or us who love individual freedom. To hell with the shallow minded liberals, they sold out over 80 years ago with the "New Deal" and have been selling the country down the river ever since.

"Long live my homeland, the home I love."

I'LL TAX YOU, TAX YOU, AND TAX YOU, TO KINGDOM COME.

All big tax and spenders are not liberals but there is no doubt they are the ones leading the herd. I'll go even farther and say that most of the people that are for higher and higher taxes are shallow and selfish. They lack the perspective and depth to understand cause and effect.

Liberals can't see the human factory in dealing with people; they think when you tax the hell out of a person it ends there. They don't understand the relativity effect. They either don't understand or don't care that when you raise taxes it always changes behavior, what is that if not selfish.

They don't understand that today even the middle income folks has to spend every red cent trying too keeping up. They don't understand the money the government is taking and squandering is not kept in that person's community providing a livelihood for some hard working soul.

Liberals think someone like me is mean, cold, and uncaring, wrong. They think someone like me is against helping the poor, wrong. I'm against conditioning the poor to be a dependent. The liberals have it backward with helping the poor.

The liberals believe in helping the poor first and then begging them to help themselves, whereas I believe in forcing the poor to try to help themselves first then I'll give the shirt off my back to someone genuine trying to survive. I understand why the liberal media and others see someone like me as uncaring and out of touch.

That is because they have never paid a severe price for survival. Throughout history almost nothing of any true lasting value has come about without some type of great struggle. Almost my whole existence has been and is still about a severe mental struggle to survive with pride and dignity.

No one has to tell me how it feels to be ridiculed, laughed at, humiliated, and counted out even to the extreme. I have experienced and know what severe self-hate and self-shame feels like, and you tell me I don't care and has no feeling for the down trodden, yet, I have survived and am still standing.

No one can convince me I have an excuse for failure. I know personally that to try and keep trying works. I know the true power of forgiveness, or I wouldn't be still standing. Please excuse me for a little self-serving on speaking about me personally but sometimes things just need to be said.

The thing about survival is there are things no one can see or understand unless they personally pay the price. That is why destiny has brought me, Freddie L. Sirmans, Sr's out of the wood works to sound the alarm. I may seemingly be unqualified, uneducated, neurotic, and counted out but sounding the alarm must go forth, regardless.

ADD ON.

The United States of America has been around over 200 years and in my opinion its survival is under the gravest threats ever. But, very few people know what the gravest threat of all is or even have the wisdom to believe it when told.

There is no sense in me beating around the bush building up suspense. "Too many people believing more government is the answer" is in my view the gravest of all threats this great country ever faced.

When you go back before the "New deal" when this "More government mentality" first got a foot in the door around 80 years ago, then it was the nuclear and extended family system that kept the hungry fed and the homeless off the streets. Since then it's been all down hill ever since. There is no sense in me going on and on trying to convince shallow minds.

I'll sum it up by saying unless taxes are cut to the bone across the board to bring back a survival need for the nuclear and extended family system there will be no saving the USA as one nation. I may not be right about a lot of things but there is no doubt that I'm right on this.

If my wisdom is ignored it really won't matter what other actions are taken the USA as we know it will not survive. There has never been and never will be a society that survived long term without a healthy nuclear and extended family system, "You can look it up." God I ask in your name save my homeland.

ADD ON.

No form of government is going to succeed without an adequate nuclear and extended family system foundation in place. A lot of people are concerned about this nation going completely socialist when it looks like the government is trying to seize absolute power.

Well, my take on this whole scenario is, dealing with a depression or going socialist would be a cakewalk to what I believe we are about to face. I believe the USA and western civilization is about to face chaos and the total breakdown of society when this global economy fails.

I base this on the fact that the welfare state system has almost completely destroyed the fabric that holds any society together. The things I'm talking about are an adequate nuclear and extended family system, an adequate moral and family value system, and an adequate emergency backup bartering capacity.

We as a nation have very little of any of those survival tools left. This is something I have been yelling about for years, still, ain't nobody listening, how sad.

ADD ON.
I see where the minimum wage is going up again. I am against any minimum wage so you know up front where I stand on the issue. Next to the welfare state I believe the minimum wage is the second most destructive thing that has been done to free enterprise in America and Western Europe.

It is like General motors building a vehicle with no reverse, which of course no one would buy. You can't have success without failure. You can't have progress without mistakes. You can't grow big without starting small. The higher the minimum wage the harder it is to start at all. We can't survive with no one providing any jobs.

The problem is very few people including

economist truly understand the foundation of economics. Almost everyone thinks cutting taxes to the bone will destroy the USA, wrong. Sure, it would be a nightmare and would destroy wealth as we know it along with all of the crud, inefficiency, moral decay, and everything else choking this country to death.

But, out of the rebirth would spring forth more greatness than ever before; otherwise the course of higher and higher taxes we are on is guaranteed doom.

The liberals for many years have been slowly tightening the screws closing off all common sense and it's now beginning to come to a head. I have said many times it is not the amount of dollars that matters; it is really the buying power of the dollar that matters.

A million dollars is not going to keep you alive if there is no food to buy or if those that have it won't sell. No amount of modern technology or materialistic creature comfort is going to matter if you don't have food to eat.

So, when you see all of this reckless printing of worthless money that is promoting a farther culture decline, it is only a matter of time before starvation raises it ugly head. Food and culture goes hand in hand and our culture is almost gone, lack of food will soon follow, whether you believe me or not. I rest my case.

A SUPER GREAT BRAIN STORMING HEALTH CARE IDEA!

This may sound radical and surprising coming from a die hard anti-big government advocate like me. Seriously, do Americans really want health care fixed or not. Well, I'll tell you how, you may not agree or like it but it's the most safe and practical approach to our life or death health care problem that I've ever heard of.

First, responsible leadership should set up in several large cities a test system similar to the veterans system, but, keep it separate by using only a token like script. Next, issue the scrip to only those below a certain income or other qualifying conditions.

After about a year or so there should be some proven results one way or another, that way we may not destroy the best health care system to ever exist in the history of mankind. Note, I didn't say the cheapest, but it is by far the best in the world. If test results are positive, sure, it could be expanded.

Still, my belief is the only way to save the USA medical health care system or even the economy itself is to kick the government completely out of it, period. If the government insist on being uncle sugar then fund public only things off to the side, but don't destroy the nation's culture, economy, and everything else in the process.

When government is out of the way natural selection market forces will never let prices or anything else get out of control. "You can't get blood out of a turnip and a chain is only as strong as its weakest link." A business can't charge more than the poor can pay, that is if the government butt out mind its own business and let the nuclear family fulfill its proper role.

THE MYTH OF FREE HEALTH CARE!

I really don't know where to start on this subject because so few have the perspective to see the big picture on this matter. Anyway, I'll just start with research and who brought modern medicine to the high level it is today. You better believe it was not a one payer communist or socialist system.

It is what's left of the good ole private enterprise free market system in the USA and its research that blazes the way in modern medicine. And another thing, big government has created this "Do for me" dependency mentality so strong that most people see the medical insurance companies as the big bad boogie man, not true, but they are guilty of paying the wrong people.

There should be a law forbidding the insurance companies from paying anyone other than who takes out the insurance that would solve ninety nine percent of the insurance blame game politics. Sure, there would be a trust factor, but the patient would always know what is coming out of his hide and it would control care giver greed.

Medical care and medical insurance should be two entirely different things with one not influencing the other. Let's brain storm and leave medical insurance out of the picture for a moment. Okay, you go to the doctor and he treats you and charges you a fee. He will expect you to pay the whole fee or as much as possible at the time.

Most people won't have the lump sum or it will cause them a severe hardship, this is where medical insurance companies found a niche. Without insurance or government involved market forces would definitely control prices. That is the true problem in the medical profession today there is no market forces to help control prices, just like throughout the economy.

What people forget is medical insurance like all businesses is profit driven. For insurance companies to survive they can only insure healthy people and hope too many won't become sick at one time. However, today most people have come to see insurance companies as a cash cow just like big government.

The doctors, nurses, and other medical workers can't work for free for you to have free health care like some have come to expect, they have to eat pay high taxes and live, too.

6 WORDS WILL DETERMINE IF USA SURVIVES OR GOES THE WAY OF THE ROMAN EMPIRE.

In 6 words I will tell you why the USA can be saved and not go the way of the Roman Empire. The 6 words are "The government shouldn't be a Provider." Sure, only on a temporary basis during an emergency the government must come to the aid of its people.

Today Very few people know what wealth is and how it is created, that is why most of the world is poor and will always be poor. Liberals have never understood wealth and still don't to this day, that is why only a miracle will save the USA with liberals in almost total control.

Wealth is the result of excess human energy in some form, that will be a foreign language to most that reads this, but it's true. A nuclear family, a state, and a nation all is made up of individuals. And in the final analysis that is the main thing that determines the health and wealth of any nation.

No sane individual is going to produce anything extra when the government takes it away and doles it out to non producers no matter the reason. Government is a destroyer of wealth and incentive; only private enterprise will produce more than enough food and wealth for the individual and the nation. Sure, some nations can prosper by selling natural resources but that is not producing and creating wealth.

What belongs to everyone in reality belongs to no one, and no caretaking will take place except by force. Whereas, there is no greater excess wealth producing forces on earth than greed and self-interest. Greed and self-interest should be bridled and harnessed but never, never completely shut down like in communist and socialist governments.

Only individual freedom and a private enterprise free market system will allow two of the most powerful motivating forces on earth greed and self-interest to generate more excess energy in wealth than you can shake a stick at. Sure, like electricity greed and self-interest can be very dangerous but they are not your enemy.

WORLD DEPENDS ON USA GOVERNMENT SURVIVAL!
LECTURE ON USA ECONOMY

Even before I became a self-made author I was preaching against big intrusive government. I have since coined our big government a welfare state beast. To the shallow it may seem like I am against all government, wrong, nothing could be further from the truth. I actually love good government, but I view big intrusive government as a threat to individual freedom.

Government is the foundation of civilization and no organized society can survive without some type of government. Today I believe the hope and survival of the whole industrialized world depends on the USA government being saved.

The USA government and the USA people are supposed to be two difference things. But today, in a sense big government spending has placed us in the same boat and tied with the same financial burdens. From the beginning when the Continental Army won our freedom from England the USA has never known anything besides individual freedom along with a free market place.

Then along came the "New deal" and the growing of big government started smothering individual freedom and our free market place. Today, after eighty years the last of our individual freedom along with our free market place is under seize by a monster size welfare state beast.

How we deal with the key word "Financial-burdens" will determine if the USA government survive or perish. Over a span of eighty years as the USA government slowly grew into this monster size welfare state it was also taking on and carrying mountain size financial-burdens.

Every financial-burden the government gladly takes on cost money, but, the sad fact is the government has no money of its own. The government can do the talk but guess who is going to do the walk.

That mean every financial-burden the government takes on will be paid out of the profit margin of business people, because there won't be any wages paid to employees to tax unless the business first make a profit. And as the government takes more and more profit fewer and fewer businesses will have enough profit left to survive on, let alone hire more workers.

The fact is the financial-burdens placed on the backs of USA business people cannot be carried much longer, the begging and borrowing has played out. Now, like bees in a hive the queen must be saved at all cost, we the people must save our USA government at all cost.

Never mind the learned experts, at this late stage there is only one way the USA government can be saved, especially with our freedom intact. The USA government must be reset back to default like the founding fathers designed it, There is no other way to save the USA government and the industrialized world.

That mean except for funding only community wise shelters, kitchens, and medical clinics the government shall be limited to defending the nation both internally and externally and doing only the bare necessary things the people can't do for themselves.

All other obligations shall be jettisoned to the private sector through privatization. Otherwise, the financial-burdens now being carried by big government will soon leave no profit margin for USA private businesses to survive on, which is still the true economically engine for the entire world economy.

That is the only way to save the USA government with our freedom intact because the global economy is going to collapse sooner than we think. If everything else fails we will still have a lean but mean USA government intact to save the industrialized world. The financial-burdens must be jettisoned or nothing will be saved so help me GOD.

You can squeeze a lemon only so many times before there is no juice left, that is a law of nature. The only way to keep our welfare state afloat is to make millions upon millions of Americans debt slaves, while others freeload. It is already happening but it is going to get a lot worse.

Stay tuned for the next episode.

LATE ENTRY:
On our welfare state beast's march to seize absolute power there is only one safeguard left to prevent its complete consolidation. That last safeguard is the U.S. Congress. As for now the U.S. Congress still has control over these nations' purse strings.

That is if they act now or very soon they can still cut taxes across the board to the bone. That is going to be the only thing that will starve this beast and stop it in its tracts. That is going to be the only thing that will prevent a complete take over of private business and absolute control.

However, I can assure you if Congress dilly dally too long they will end up as just a group of ceremonial figure heads. And our welfare state beast will have consolidated its power.

Light, lights, lights, the movie is over folks, that was the wild imagination of this neurotic writer.

Nothing I just wrote is to be taken serious as real or fact. Thank God I didn't let my imagination get too carried away. Stay tuned for future episodes.

PS: In a family or in a nation whoever is the provider is the boss, in a free society the government should be a dependent of the people, not the people a dependent of the government. Only cutting taxes to the bone across the board will put the people back in control. However, don't bet the farm on it.

FUTURE USA BLUEPRINT
Here I go again giving an imaginary analysis that I dreamed up with no real life information to back me up. As I sit back in my recliner and watch the way our liberal welfare state beast is grabbing power and flexing its muscles I am almost in awe of its raw display of power. Or course I am one hundred and eighty degrees opposed to what is taking place.

I too believe the USA economy is headed toward a collapse, but I believe the best way to save our freedom and country is through mass tax cuts across the board. And get government completely out of the market place then deflation and the free market place will save this great country with our freedom intact.

I believe the great thinkers along with the movers and shakers within the power structure of this country know that the USA economy is on its last lap. I think the million dollar question was can the USA survive an economic collapse as a free market place nation, or should the government have total control over everything.

I think they have decided the government must seize total control over private business and everything else. I think the "Blueprint" is the government must have absolute junta like power for the USA to survive an economic collapse. Lord God I beg in your name, save our great nation.

IS THE USA DUMB, STUPID, OR JUST PLAIN NAIVE?

We have all of our survival eggs in one basket; I think that is dumb, stupid, or just plain naive. No matter what name you may call me it won't prove me wrong. Freedom in the USA will soon be over if good men of wisdom continue to say nothing.

Like a broken record as long as I have the freedom to I'm going to stay stuck on shouting to all who will listen that the USA must cut taxes to the bone across the board. I believe there is no way freedom can survive very much longer in the USA unless taxes are cut to the bone across the board.

I base this on a lack of good judgment and wisdom because our welfare state has destroyed good judgment in 95 percent of the American voters. No government with a strong survival instinct and proper judgment would allow all of its survival eggs to be in just one basket.

Good men took the course of least resistance and allowed a "New Deal' baby to slowly grow and take away our nations independent frontier like spirit. Now, with our welfare state beast planted firmly in control as a social and nuclear family provider there is very little power the average Joe/Jane has except to vote.

And that is practically worthless, because he lacks the judgment to vote for what is in the long term best interest of his country in my opinion. Today the survival of over 300 million Americans are in only one basket our sugar daddy welfare state provider, and when it collapses there won't be any order, except out of the barrel of a gun.

There will never be enough tax dollars to ever satisfy our welfare states appetite. That means it is only a matter of time before our welfare state tax bleeds us to death. When that happens it will mean millions upon millions of dependent Americans are going to be left physical and culturally unprepared for survival.

That is why no matter what they call me as long as I have breath in my body I'm going to continue to plead, yell, turn flips, or whatever to stress the dangers of not rebuilding our nuclear and extended family system, even if no one ever listens. The following No's used to be three additional egg baskets, but not anymore.

We have almost no strong nuclear and extended family system left, especially among African Americans. We have almost no strong moral and family values left, a kid can hardly use a computer without being exposed to smut. We have no adequate emergency bartering capacity with small farmers and home gardeners left to give this nation time to save our freedom if a calamity strikes.

Instead good men for years has stood by and let the shallow minded liberals slowly destroy this great nation with this welfare state. Sure, if taxes were cut to the bone across the board it will cause much, much hardship and suffering, but it will give this great nation a fighting chance to survive with our freedom intact.

Otherwise, we can sell the last of our soul and pride and this welfare state is still going to collapse. If we don't act first and Mother Nature has to steps in herself to enforce its natural selection law we will have no control and that could mean back to the Stone Age.

One positive, is a tax cut to the bone across the board will reset government back to default which is the way the founding fathers designed it to be. The USA government was never designed to be a social and nuclear family provider.

The USA government was designed to protect the nation from both internal and external threats, and do only the bare necessary things the citizens couldn't do for themselves. However, since the welfare state has made millions upon millions of citizens solely dependent on the government for survival they can never be abandoned.

Therefore, added to governments responsibility to protect the nation from internal and external threats, it now has an additional duty to provide community shelters, kitchens, and medical clinics, but very little else. The reason for little else is the Nuclear and extended family must be rebuilt at all cost and that can never happen unless there is a survival need for it.

A woman must have a survival need for a man, and a man must have a survival need for a woman for any society to survive long term. With the government out of private business and out of the way, then like a Phoenix rising up out of the ashes private enterprise with entrepreneurs will save our great country with our freedom intact.

On the other hand, to continue down the doomsday road we are on by trying to keep tax feeding our welfare state beast we are going to end up losing our freedom our country and everything else when this beast finish taxing us to death.

Like I've said before our welfare state is going to soon fall from its own weight because with the printing presses humming 24-7 it still won't be enough to keep this ferocious tax eating beast fed. Our greatest threat is to keep masses of people from starving, but never under estimate the American spirit. The old American frontier spirit is not all dead, yet.

We will survive. Excuse me for getting a little long winded. Thank you God for my life, health, and strength.....

LATE ENTRY:
It is a fact the higher all taxes across the board the fewer and fewer businesses are

going to make a profit. It is not just me saying it; it is nature's law of natural selection in action. The liberals have been willing to beg, borrow, and steal to feed and support the appetite of our monster size welfare state beast.

We have sold down the river our soul, our manufacturing base, and just about everything else all to support this liberal created welfare state beast. Now, almost like a junkie on the streets, there is nothing we won't do to get this beast his fix.

Most people that read my writing see me as a lowly pest that can be swatted away anytime, but the liberals know better. The liberals see me as a real threat to their God and master, the welfare state beast. The reason is because I am coming in under the radar and landing some small but deadly strategic blows.

God I ask in your name, save our great nation.

LECTURE ON THE UNITED STATES ECONOMY:

As a lone writer let me say up front I don't expect many people to agree with me on hardly anything I write. In fact even myself, I hope I'm wrong about most of the things I write about. Sure, some people think I'm an idiot stuck on stupid because like a broken record I keep repeating across the board cut taxes to the bone, cut taxes to the bone.

I don't just believe it I know it for a fact that our freedom and economy will never be save unless taxes is cut to the bone. I also know that the law of natural selection is going to make it impossible to prevent the United States economy from collapsing unless taxes are cut to the bone.

I believe the whole USA economy is out of balanced and top heavy with too high taxes already. I believe all of the actions our management economists is doing is just buying time and holding on to the fantasy that we can keep paying for this monster size welfare state that is sucking the freedom and life blood out of this great nation.

I'm able to look past all of the fog and distractions and bore right to the heart of our economic problem. Now, forget about all of this other nonsense and focus on the thing that really matters, and that is profit, profit, and more profit if you want a successful free market place.

It all starts with a profit and unless a nation has masses upon masses of business people making a profits the government ain't gonna have nothing to tax. A successful free market place economy is the only economical system that can feed all of its people and more.

No other system even comes close. I'm going to clue you in on something right now, mass starving and hunger will be coming our way, it always does, you just wait until our welfare state beast finish destroying our private businesses and our free market place.

Yes, printing all of this worthless money is insane, but the thing that caused all of this sky is the limit inflation that is killing us is from government giving out free money on an individual basis. Doing that subsides price rising and allows merchants to keep raising the cost of living on everyone.

If not for that it would be impossible for prices or the cost of living to go higher than the masses of poor could pay out of pocket. And believe it or not the poor and the nation would be far better off today. Without government giving out money on an individual basis the poor would quickly rebuild the nuclear family to survive like all throughout history.

Worldwide the welfare state nations has left ninety five percent of its people too shallow with weak survival instincts to know that we can't survive as civilized societies when the global economy soon collapses. The free individual hand out act not only inflated our currency out of sight, it destroyed the need to depend on the nuclear family.

Now, if we lose our job half of us will end up homeless. I close for now, I don't want to get too long winded, stay tuned for the next episode.

Self-made writer Freddie L. Sirmans, Sr. is an original creative thinker with supernatural like wisdom. Take heed.

VALDOSTA, GEORGIA USA
WEBSITE: FLSirmans.com

THE END